C000230904

LITTLE BOOK OF
WISDOM

HarperCollins*Publishers*
1 London Bridge Street
London SE1 9GF

www.harpercollins.co.uk

HarperCollins*Publishers*
Macken House
39/40 Mayor Street Upper
Dublin 1
D01 C9W8
Ireland

First published by HarperCollins*Publishers* in 2023

1 3 5 7 9 10 8 6 4 2

Compiled by Andrea Kirk Assaf
Cover illustrations: Photo frame © Shutterstock;
background texture and portrait silhouette © iStock
Interior illustrations: Frame and flourishes © iStock, house © Shutterstock
Cover and interior design by e-Digital Design

A catalogue record for this book is available from the British Library

ISBN 978-0-00-856767-5

Printed and bound in Bosnia and Herzegovina

MIX
Paper | Supporting
responsible forestry
FSC™ C007454

This book is produced from
independently certified FSC™
paper to ensure responsible
forest management.

Find out more about HarperCollins and the environment at
www.harpercollins.co.uk/green

Jane Austen's
LITTLE BOOK OF
WISDOM

Words on Love, Life, Society and Literature

COMPILED BY ANDREA KIRK ASSAF

WILLIAM
COLLINS

Indulge your imagination in every possible flight.

Pride and Prejudice

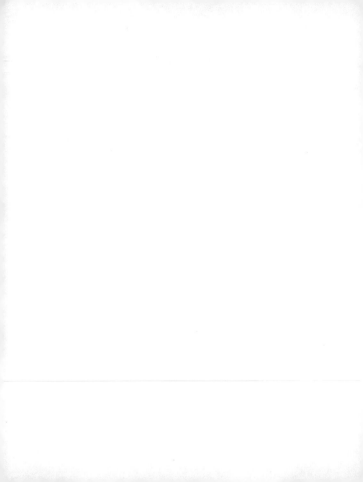

Contents

Introduction

If you're holding this little book in your hands, it may be presumed that you are already a devotee of Miss Austen or perhaps you are eager to become one through familiarizing yourself with this collection of her famous quotes of wit and wisdom. Whichever category you fall into, you are in for a treat! Whether you choose a quote a day to reflect upon or devour it all in a single delicious hour, when you close the final page, you will have experienced a broad glimpse into the world and mind of a fascinating and very funny lady.

Some of the quotes here are Austen's own direct thoughts, such as those from her prayers, poems, and amusing, self-deprecating personal letters, most of which were addressed to her best friend and sister, Cassandra. All the rest come from the mouths of her most memorable fictional characters.

Why does Jane Austen continue to attract such a loyal and ever increasing number of fans who never seem to tire of new film adaptations of her novels? Beyond the compelling characters she creates, such as the snobbish yet lovable Emma, or the swoon-worthy yet haughty Mr. Darcy, there are the attractive gems of humor and insight that Austen offers us through them. This is what this little book offers you, dear reader: a tantalizing taste of Jane's mind and soul on themes dearest to her heart.

Through her words and characters, Jane becomes a friend, mentor, and lover to us. Enchanted by the world and stories she brings to our inner lives, we want to know something meaningful about this brilliant, sharp, and jocular woman who lived a rather undramatic life and died too soon.

It is perhaps surprising that, in our overstimulated, frenetically paced world, an author as subtle and slow-paced (by modern standards) as Jane Austen would continue to inspire such passion and loyalty among readers. English editor, essayist, and writer Ronald Blythe, who edited one edition of *Emma*, gives us an answer: 'Jane Austen can in fact get more drama out of morality than most other writers can get from shipwreck, battle, murder, or mayhem.'

Morality. There's a theme that runs through all of Austen's novels. Virtue must triumph over vice, the heroine must have her hero, love must be sought and won, wrongs must be righted. Jane's moral dramas are attired in rather lovely clothing from the wardrobe of the world she knew best—the landed gentry. Born into the lower end of the educated gentry class of the Georgian era, Jane's social position between the nobility and the working class allowed her to observe all layers of the English hierarchical stratum. She is well known for having applied this perceptive knowledge in her satirical criticism of certain aspects of polite Georgian society. The Christian humanist theme that runs throughout, clothed in humor and delightful narrative, is the inner worth of an individual—not based upon social status that is an accident of birth, or upon outward appearances, but rather upon true virtue, often that which is earned through some sort of trial.

Jane may have drawn upon the experience of her own personal trials when crafting that of her heroes' and heroines'. One trial with which Austen fans will no doubt be very familiar, is that of her failed romance with Tom Lefroy. Austen was entirely prepared to accept an anticipated offer of marriage, as she wrote in a letter to her sister Cassandra, only to have him disappear from her company forever, and see him eventually married to an heiress. Years later, Jane did accept an offer of marriage from a wealthy family friend, but thought better of it by morning. Cassandra suffered a similar fate when her fiancé died of yellow fever while abroad trying to earn money for the marriage. Neither sister ever married and they lived the rest of their lives together, first in their parents' homes and later in property belonging to their brothers.

The questions 'Who will the girl marry, and will it be a good match?' appear in all of Austen's novels. But Jane herself left these questions unanswered in her own life, as did her sister. Her financial dependency upon her relations is another theme that has often been compared to that of her characters, such as the plight of Elinor and Marianne in *Sense and Sensibility*. And yet the lack of resolution in Jane's romantic life may actually be the reason we are able to enjoy reading about the happy resolutions in the lives of her characters today. Her mother and sister assumed the greater majority of the daily housekeeping, thereby granting Jane the time and space necessary to pen her novels. Her brothers provided her with housing and financial support, particularly necessary at a time when the profession of novelist was not lucrative, especially for women. Jane neither received fortune nor great fame during her lifetime, no doubt exacerbated by her decision—common at the time—to publish her novels under the name 'By A Lady' (though her authorship was an open secret).

There are more than enough interpretations and analyses available for fans seeking to know the 'real Jane,' but perhaps her own brother summarized her enduring charisma best in the epitaph her penned for her grave marker in Winchester Cathedral, England:

The benevolence of her heart, the sweetness of her temper and the extraordinary endowments of her mind obtained the regard of all who knew her, and the warmest love of her intimate connections.

This little book invites us to become one of those intimate connections as we ponder the same themes of life she repeatedly returned to in her novels, poems, letters, and prayers—love and longing, friendship, faith, virtue, and more. In the Reader's Journal at the back of this book, we might create our own words of wisdom inspired by our friend Jane, or perhaps pen a love note to be discovered by our own Mr. Darcy or Miss Bennet . . .

Happy reading!

Andrea Kirk Assaf

'If I loved you less, I might be able to talk about it more.'

Emma

Her heart did whisper that he had done it for her.

Pride and Prejudice

'Of course I love her, but there are as many forms of love as there are moments in time.'

Mansfield Park

'There is no charm equal to tenderness of heart.'

Emma

It was gratitude; gratitude, not merely for having once loved her, but for loving her still well enough to forgive all the petulance and acrimony of her manner in rejecting him, and all the unjust accusations accompanying her rejection.

Pride and Prejudice

'Whom are you going to dance with?' asked Mr. Knightley.

She hesitated a moment and then replied, 'With you, if you will ask me.'

'Will you?' said he, offering his hand.

'Indeed I will. You have shown that you can dance, and you know we are not really so much brother and sister as to make it at all improper.'

'Brother and sister! No, indeed.'

Emma

At length the day is come on which I am to flirt my last with Tom Lefroy, and when you receive this it will be over. My tears flow at the melancholy idea.

Excerpt from a personal letter

'Were I to fall in love, indeed, it would be a different thing; but I have never been in love; it is not my way, or my nature; and I do not think I ever shall.'

Emma

'Where the heart is really attached,
I know very well how little one can
be pleased with the attention of anybody else.'

Northanger Abbey

She was one of those, who, having, once begun, would be always in love.

Emma

'Fanny! You are killing me!'
    'No man dies of love but on the stage, Mr. Crawford.'

Mansfield Park

To be fond of dancing was a certain step
towards falling in love.

Pride and Prejudice

Thus much indeed he was obliged to acknowledge—that he had been constant unconsciously, nay unintentionally; that he had meant to forget her, and believed it to be done. He had imagined himself indifferent, when he had only been angry; and he had been unjust to her merits, because he had been a sufferer from them.

Persuasion

Had I been in love, I could not have been more wretchedly blind. But vanity, not love, has been my folly.

Pride and Prejudice

They were brought together by mutual affection, with the warmest approbation of their real friends; their intimate knowledge of each other seemed to make their happiness certain.

Sense and Sensibility

'Mr. Knightley, if I have not spoken, it is because I am afraid I will awaken myself from this dream.'

Emma

'If you will thank me,' he replied, 'let it be for yourself alone. That the wish of giving happiness to you might add force to the other inducements which led me on, I shall not attempt to deny. But your family owe me nothing. Much as I respect them, I believe I thought only of you.'

Pride and Prejudice

They had no conversation together, no intercourse but what the commonest civility required. Once so much to each other! Now nothing!

Persuasion

'Perhaps it is our imperfections that make us so perfect for one another.'

Emma

'Dare not say that man forgets sooner than woman, that his love has an earlier death. I have loved none but you. Unjust I may have been, weak and resentful I have been, but never inconstant.'

Persuasion

'My affections and wishes are unchanged; but one word from you will silence me on this subject forever.'

Pride and Prejudice

'I would rather be overturned by him, than driven safely by anybody else.'

Persuasion

She longed to know what at the moment was passing in his mind, in what manner he thought of her, and whether, in defiance of everything, she was still dear to him. Perhaps he had been civil only because he felt himself at ease; yet there had been that in his voice which was not like ease.

Pride and Prejudice

There are such beings in the world—perhaps one in a thousand—as the creature you and I should think perfection; where grace and spirit are united to worth, where the manners are equal to the heart and understanding; but such a person may not come in your way, or, if he does, he may not be the eldest son of a man of fortune, the near relation of your particular friend, and belonging to your own county.

Excerpt from a personal letter

She learned romance as she grew older: the natural sequel of an unnatural beginning.

Persuasion

I think it ought not to be set down as certain
that a man must be acceptable to every
woman he may happen to like himself.

Mansfield Park

'My mind was more agreeably engaged. I have been meditating on the very great pleasure which a pair of fine eyes in the face of a pretty woman can bestow.'

Pride and Prejudice

For though a very few hours spent in hard labour of incessant talking will dispatch more subjects than can really be in common between any two rational creatures, yet with lovers it is different. Between them no subject is finished, no communication is even made, till it has been made at least twenty times over.

Sense and Sensibility

'I cannot fix on the hour, or the spot, or the look, or the words, which laid the foundation. It is too long ago. I was in the middle before I knew that I had begun.'

Pride and Prejudice

'You pierce my soul. I am half agony,
half hope ... I have loved none but you.'

Persuasion

'I was simple enough to think, that because my faith was plighted to another, there could be no danger in my being with you; and that the consciousness of my engagement was to keep my heart as safe and sacred as my honour.'

Sense and Sensibility

'I offer myself to you again with a heart
even more your own than when you
almost broke it, eight years and a half ago.'

Persuasion

Whether he had felt more of pain or of pleasure in seeing her she could not tell, but he certainly had not seen her with composure.

Pride and Prejudice

'If I could but know his heart, everything would become easy.'

Sense and Sensibility

'There is safety in reserve, but no attraction. One cannot love a reserved person.'

Emma

'It is not time or opportunity that is to determine intimacy;—it is disposition alone. Seven years would be insufficient to make some people acquainted with each other, and seven days are more than enough for others.'

Sense and Sensibility

'Dare not say that man forgets sooner than woman, that his love has an earlier death.'

Persuasion

'Always resignation and acceptance. Always prudence and honour and duty. Elinor, where is your heart?'

Sense and Sensibility

'Do anything rather than marry without affection.'

Pride and Prejudice

'The more I know of the world, the more
I am convinced that I shall never see a
man whom I can really love. I require so much!'

Sense and Sensibility

'Could there be finer symptoms? Is not general incivility the very essence of love?'

Pride and Prejudice

'A man does not recover from such devotion of the heart to such a woman! He ought not; he does not.'

Persuasion

She had probably alienated love by the helplessness and fretfulness of a fearful temper, or been unreasonable in wanting a larger share than anyone among so many could deserve.

Mansfield Park

Husbands and wives generally understand when opposition will be vain.

Persuasion

'In vain I have struggled. It will not do.
My feelings will not be repressed.
You must allow me to tell you how ardently
I admire and love you.'

Pride and Prejudice

When any two young people take it into their heads to marry, they are pretty sure by perseverance to carry their point, be they ever so poor, or ever so imprudent, or ever so little likely to be necessary to each other's ultimate comfort.

Persuasion

'Beware how you give your heart.'

Northanger Abbey

'No man is offended by another man's admiration of the woman he loves; it is the woman only who can make it a torment.'

Northanger Abbey

' I was quiet, but I was not blind.'

Mansfield Park

Their eyes instantly met, and the cheeks of both were overspread with the deepest blush.

Pride and Prejudice

'This sensation of listlessness, weariness,
stupidity, this disinclination to sit
down and employ myself, this feeling of
everything's being dull and insipid about
the house! I must be in love; I should be the
oddest creature in the world if I were not.'

Emma

[T] here was little to distress them beyond the want of graciousness and warmth.

Persuasion

'The very first moment I beheld him, my heart was irrevocably gone.'

Northanger Abbey

'To love is to burn, to be on fire.'

Sense and Sensibility

There could have been no two hearts so open, no tastes so similar, no feelings so in unison.

Persuasion

'He will make you happy, Fanny;
I know he will make you happy;
but you will make him everything.'

Mansfield Park

She began now to comprehend that he was exactly the man who, in disposition and talents, would most suit her. His understanding and temper, though unlike her own, would have answered all her wishes.

It was a union that must have been to the advantage of both: by her ease and liveliness, his mind might have been softened, his manners improved; and from his judgment, information, and knowledge of the world, she must have received benefit of greater importance.

Pride and Prejudice

'My real purpose was to see you, and to judge, if I could, whether I might ever hope to make you love me.'

Pride and Prejudice

'I may have lost my heart, but not my
self-control.'

Emma

Nothing can be compared to the misery
of being bound without love.

Excerpt from a personal letter

'We are all fools in love.'

Pride and Prejudice

'I come here with no expectations, only to profess, now that I am at liberty to do so, that my heart is and always will be yours.'

Sense and Sensibility

They walked on, without knowing in what direction. There was too much to be thought, and felt, and said, for attention to any other objects.

Pride and Prejudice

'Then I examined my own heart.
   And there you were. Never, I fear,
to be removed.'

Emma

To you I shall say, as I have often said before: Do not be in a hurry. The right man will come at last.

Excerpt from a personal letter

By not one of the circle was he listened to with such unbroken, unalloyed enjoyment as by his wife, who was really extremely happy to see him, and whose feelings were so warmed by his sudden arrival [...]

It was so agreeable to her to see him again, and hear him talk, to have her ear amused

and her whole comprehension filled by his
narratives, that she began particularly to feel
how dreadfully she must have missed him,
and how impossible it would have been for
her to bear a lengthened absence.

Mansfield Park

Friendship

Sitting with her on Sunday evening—a
Swet Sunday evening—the very time of all
others when if a friend is at hand the heart
must be opened, and everything told . . .

Mansfield Park

'But people themselves alter so much, that there is something new to be observed in them forever.'

Pride and Prejudice

'She is probably by this time as tired of me, as I am of her; but as she is too polite and I am too civil to say so, our letters are still as frequent and affectionate as ever, and our attachment as firm and sincere as when it first commenced.'

Love and Friendship

Friendship is certainly the finest balm for
the pangs of disappointed love.

Northanger Abbey

A ngelic Woman! past my power to praise
In Language meet, thy Talents, Temper, mind.
Thy solid Worth, thy captivating Grace!
Thou friend and ornament of Humankind!

Excerpted from the poem 'To the Memory of Mrs. Lefroy
who died Dec. 16—my birthday'

'I will not torment myself any longer by remaining among friends whose society it is impossible for me now to enjoy.'

Sense and Sensibility

W hich of all my important nothings
shall I tell you first?

Excerpt from a personal letter

'Business, you know, may bring money, but friendship hardly ever does.'

Emma

'Now, if I were to hear anybody speak slightingly of you, I should fire up in a moment.'

Northanger Abbey

'*You* want to tell me, and I have no objection to hearing it.' That was invitation enough.

Pride and Prejudice

'You are in a melancholy humour, and fancy that any one unlike yourself must be happy. But remember that the pain of parting from friends will be felt by everybody at times, whatever be their education or state. Know your own happiness. You want nothing but patience—or give it a more fascinating name, call it hope.'

Sense and Sensibility

'There is nothing so bad as parting with one's friends. One seems too forlorn without them.'

Pride and Prejudice

Still he could not see her suffer, without the desire of giving her relief. It was a remainder of former sentiment; it was an impulse of pure, though unacknowledged friendship; it was a proof of his own warm and amiable heart, which she could not contemplate without emotions so compounded of pleasure and pain, that she knew not which prevailed.

Persuasion

I do not want people to be very agreeable,
as it saves me the trouble of liking them a
great deal.

Excerpt from a personal letter

'There is nothing I would not do for those who are really my friends. I have no notion of loving people by halves, it is not my nature. My attachments are always excessively strong.'

Northanger Abbey

'I will tell you truths while I can: satisfied with proving myself your friend by very faithful counsel, and trusting that you will some time or other do me greater justice than you can do now.'

Emma

'To me, she was in the place of a parent.'

Persuasion

'It is such a happiness when good people get together.'

Emma

Home &
Society

It is a truth universally acknowledged, that a
single man in possession of a good fortune,
must be in want of a wife.

Pride and Prejudice

Nothing was so likely to do her good as a little quiet cheerfulness at home.

Persuasion

'She always travels with her own sheets; an excellent precaution.'

Emma

Our time was most delightfully spent, in mutual Protestations of Friendship, and in vows of unalterable Love, in which we were secure from being interrupted, by intruding and disagreeable Visitors, as Augustus and Sophia had on their first Entrance in the Neighborhood, taken due care to inform the surrounding Families, that as their happiness centered wholly in themselves, they wished for no other society.

Love and Friendship

'Happiness in marriage is entirely a matter of chance. If the dispositions of the parties are ever so well known to each other or ever so similar beforehand, it does not advance their felicity in the least. It is better to know as little as possible of the defects of the person with whom you are about to pass your life.'

Pride and Prejudice

'I pay very little regard to what any young person says on the subject of marriage. If they profess a disinclination for it, I only set it down that they have not yet seen the right person.'

Mansfield Park

'Marriage is indeed a maneuvering business.'

Mansfield Park

'Nobody, who has not been in the interior of a family, can say what the difficulties of any individual of that family may be.'

Emma

'Ah! There is nothing like staying at home for real comfort. Nobody can be more devoted to home than I am.'

Emma

'He is a gentleman; I am a gentleman's daughter; So far, we are equal.'

Pride and Prejudice

'Wherever you are you should always be contented, but especially at home, because there you must spend the most of your time.'

Northanger Abbey

'There are few people whom I really love, and still fewer of whom I think well. The more I see of the world, the more am I dissatisfied with it; and every day confirms my belief of the inconsistency of all human characters, and of the little dependence that can be placed on the appearance of merit or sense.'

Pride and Prejudice

The many comforts that await
  Our Chawton home, how much we find
Already in it, to our mind;
And how convinced, that when complete
It will all other Houses beat
The ever have been made or mended,

With rooms concise, or rooms distended.
You'll find us very snug next year,
Perhaps with Charles and Fanny near,
For now it often does delight us
To fancy them just over-right us.

Excerpt from the poem 'My Dearest Frank, I Wish You Joy'

'A man would always wish to give a woman
a better home than the one he takes her
from; and he who can do it, where there is
no doubt of her regard, must, I think, be the
happiest of mortals.'

Emma

We are to have a tiny party here tonight;
I hate tiny parties—they force one
into constant exertion.

Excerpt from a personal letter

However little known the feelings or views of such a man may be on his first entering a neighborhood, this truth is so well fixed in the minds of the surrounding families that he is considered as the rightful property of some one or other of their daughters.

Pride and Prejudice

'It is so delightful to have an evening now and then to oneself.'

Northanger Abbey

'For what do we live, but to make sport
for our neighbors, and laugh at them
in our turn?'

Pride and Prejudice

'One half of the world cannot understand
the pleasures of the other.'

Emma

'My idea of good company . . . is the company of clever, well-informed people, who have a great deal of conversation; that is what I call good company.'

'You are mistaken,' said he gently, 'that is not good company, that is the best.'

Emma

When stretch'd on one's bed
    With a fierce-throbbing head,
Which precludes alike thought or repose,
How little one cares
For the grandest affairs
That may busy the world as it goes!

'Oh! who can ever be tired of Bath?'

Northanger Abbey

'[E]very man is surrounded by a
neighborhood of voluntary spies.'

Northanger Abbey

On Being
a Woman

'I hate to hear you talk about all women as if they were fine ladies instead of rational creatures. None of us want to be in calm waters all our lives.'

Persuasion

'Every neighborhood should have a great lady.'

Sandition

'You may ask questions which I shall not
choose to answer.'

Pride and Prejudice

'Run mad as often as you choose, but do not faint.'

Love and Friendship

Women of that class have great opportunities, and if they are intelligent may be well worth listening to. Such varieties of human nature as they are in the habit of witnessing! And it is not merely in its follies that they are read; for they see it occasionally under every circumstance that can be most interesting or affecting.

What instances must pass before them
of ardent, disinterested, self-denying
attachment, of heroism, fortitude, patience,
resignation—of all the sacrifices that ennoble
us most. A sick chamber may often furnish the
worth of volumes.

Persuasion

Where youth and diffidence are united,
it requires uncommon steadiness of
reason to resist the attraction of being called
the most charming girl in the world.

Northanger Abbey

'I hope I do justice to all that is felt by you, and by those who resemble you. God forbid that I should undervalue the warm and faithful feelings of any of my fellow-creatures! I should deserve utter contempt if I dared to suppose that true attachment and constancy were known only by woman.'

Persuasion

'Good-humored, unaffected girls, will not do for a man who has been used to sensible women. They are two distinct orders of being.'

Mansfield Park

'Men have had every advantage of us in telling their own story. Education has been theirs in so much higher a degree; the pen has been in their hands. I will not allow books to prove anything.'

Persuasion

As for admiration, it was always very welcome when it came, but she did not depend on it.

Northanger Abbey

'A single woman with a very narrow income must be a ridiculous, disagreeable old maid—the proper sport of boys and girls; but a single woman of good fortune is always respectable, and may be as sensible and pleasant as anybody else.'

Emma

'An engaged woman is always more agreeable than a disengaged. She is satisfied with herself. Her cares are over, and she feels that she may exert all her powers of pleasing without suspicion. All is safe with a lady engaged; no harm can be done.'

Mansfield Park

Another world must be unfurled,
Another language known,
Ere tongue or sound can publish round
Her charms of flesh and bone.

'All the privilege I claim for my own sex (it is not a very enviable one: you need not covet it), is that of loving longest, when existence or when hope is gone!'

Persuasion

A young woman in love always looks 'like Patience on a monument Smiling at Grief.'

Northanger Abbey

'If I know myself [...] mine is an active, busy mind, with a great many independent resources; and I do not perceive why I should be more in want of employment at forty or fifty than one-and-twenty.

Woman's usual occupations of hand and mind will be as open to me then as they are now; or with no important variation. If I draw less, I shall read more; if I give up music, I shall take to carpet-work.'

Emma

She was sensible and clever, but eager in everything; her sorrows, her joys, could have no moderation.

Sense and Sensibility

'Nursing does not belong to a man, it is not his province. A sick child is always the mother's property, her own feelings generally make it so.'

Persuasion

'There are certainly not so many men of large fortune in the world, as there are pretty women to deserve them.'

Mansfield Park

'I am determined that only the deepest love will induce me into matrimony. So, I shall end an old maid, and teach your ten children to embroider cushions and play their instruments very ill.'

Pride and Prejudice

'I am very strong. Nothing ever fatigues me but doing what I do not like.'

Mansfield Park

I see her here, with all her smiles benign,
  Her looks of eager Love, her accents sweet.
That voice and Countenance almost divine!
Expression, Harmony, alike complete.

Excerpt from the poem 'To the Memory of Mrs. Lefroy

who died Dec. 16—my birthday'

'And yet she was a happy woman, and a woman whom no one named without good will.'

Emma

'If adventures will not befall a young lady in her own village, she must seek them abroad.'

Northanger Abbey

'I do not think I ever opened a book in my life which had not something to say upon woman's inconstancy. Songs and proverbs, all talk of woman's fickleness. But perhaps you will say, these were all written by men.'

Persuasion

She was stronger alone; and her own good sense so well supported her, that her firmness was as unshaken, her appearance of cheerfulness as invariable, as, with regrets so poignant and so fresh, it was possible for them to be.

Sense and Sensibility

'[N]obody is afraid of her: that is a great charm.'

Emma

'I always deserve the best treatment, because
I never put up with any other.'

Emma

'Do not consider me now as an elegant female, intending to play you, but as a rational creature, speaking the truth from her heart.'

Pride and Prejudice

To look almost pretty, is an acquisition of higher delight to a girl who has been looking plain the first fifteen years of her life, than a beauty from her cradle can ever imagine.

Northanger Abbey

She was not often invited to join in the conversation of the others, nor did she desire it. Her own thoughts and reflections were habitually her best companions.

Mansfield Park

'Blessed with so many resources within myself the world was not necessary to me. I could do very well without it.'

Emma

From fifteen to seventeen she was in training for a heroine.

Northanger Abbey

'There, I will stake my last like a woman of spirit. No cold prudence for me. I am not born to sit still and do nothing. If I lose the game, it shall not be from not striving for it.'

Mansfield Park

'A woman is not to marry a man merely
because she is asked, or because he is
attached to her, and can write a tolerable letter.'

Emma

'A lady's imagination is very rapid; it jumps from admiration to love, from love to matrimony in a moment.'

Pride and Prejudice

'Men of sense, whatever you may choose to say, do not want silly wives.'

Emma

'In nine cases out of ten, a woman had better show more affection than she feels.'

Pride and Prejudice

'Woman is fine for her own satisfaction alone. No man will admire her the more, no woman will like her the better for it. Neatness and fashion are enough for the former, and a something of shabbiness or impropriety will be most endearing to the latter.'

Northanger Abbey

'You showed me how insufficient were all my pretensions to please a woman worthy of being pleased.'

Pride and Prejudice

'I lay it down as a general rule, Harriet, that if a woman doubts as to whether she should accept a man or not, she certainly ought to refuse him.'

Emma

'Pray, pray be composed' cried Elinor, 'and do not betray what you feel to every body present.'

Sense and Sensibility

'Everybody allows that the talent of writing agreeable letters is peculiarly female.'

Northanger Abbey

'Give a girl an education and introduce her properly into the world and ten to one she has the means of settling well without further expense to anybody.'

Mansfield Park

Life, Death,
and Spirituality

'Life seems but a quick succession of busy nothings.'

Mansfield Park

'Tis past and gone—We meet no more below.
Short is the Cheat of Fancy o'er the Tomb.
Oh! might I hope to equal Bliss to go!
To meet thee Angel! in thy future home!

Excerpt from the poem 'To the Memory of Mrs. Lefroy
who died Dec. 16—my birthday'

'It will, I believe, be everywhere found, that as the clergy are, or are not what they ought to be, so are the rest of the nation.'

Mansfield Park

Life could do nothing for her, beyond giving time for a better preparation for death; and that was given.

Sense and Sensibility

May we now, and on each return of night, consider how the past day has been spent by us, what have been our prevailing thoughts, words, and actions during it.

Excerpt from a personal prayer

You may not live another year,
All's mortal here below.

Excerpt from the poem 'Oh! Mr Best You're Very Bad'

The day returns again, my natal day;
    What mix'd emotions with the
Thought arise!
Beloved friend, four years have pass'd away
Since thou wert snatch'd forever from our eyes.
The day, commemorative of my birth

Bestowing Life and Light and Hope on me,
Brings back the hour which was thy last
on Earth.
Oh! bitter pang of torturing Memory!

Excerpt from the poem 'To the Memory of Mrs. Lefroy
who died Dec. 16—my birthday'

For all whom we love and value, for every friend and connection, we equally pray; however divided and far asunder, we know that we are alike before thee, and under thine eye.

Excerpt from a personal prayer

But the Providence of God has restored me—& may I be more fit to appear before him when I *am* summoned, than I should have been now!

Excerpt from a personal letter

Give us grace, Almighty Father, so to pray, as to deserve to be heard, to address thee with our hearts, as with our lips. Thou art everywhere present, from thee no secret can be hid. May the knowledge of this, teach us to fix our thoughts on thee, with reverence and devotion that we pray not in vain.

Excerpt from a personal prayer

Her's is the Energy of Soul sincere.
Her Christian Spirit ignorant to feign,
Seeks but to comfort, heal, enlighten, cheer,
Confer a pleasure, or prevent a pain.

Excerpt from 'To the Memory of Mrs. Lefroy
who died Dec. 16—my birthday'

May the comforts of every day, be thankfully felt by us, may they prompt a willing obedience of thy commandments and a benevolent spirit toward every fellow-creature.

Excerpt from a personal prayer

'I have been thinking over the past, and trying impartially to judge of the right and wrong, I mean with regard to myself.'

Persuasion

The Arts,
Intellect, and
Nature

A mind lively and at ease, can do with seeing nothing, and can see nothing that does not answer.

Emma

I t is better to write than to speak.

Excerpt from the poem 'Miss Lloyd has now went to Miss Green'

Such a letter was not to be soon recovered from . . . Every moment rather brought fresh agitation. It was an overpowering happiness.

Persuasion

E xpect a most agreeable letter, for not being overburdened with subject (having nothing at all to say), I shall have no check to my genius from beginning to end.

Excerpt from a personal letter

'Oh!' cried Marianne, 'with what transporting sensations have I formerly seen them fall! How have I delighted, as I walked, to see them driven in showers about me by the wind! What feelings have they, the season, the air altogether inspired!

Now there is no one to regard them. They are seen only as a nuisance, swept hastily off, and driven as much as possible from the sight.'

'It is not everyone,' said Elinor, 'who has your passion for dead leaves.'

Sense and Sensibility

I could no more write a [historical] romance than an epic poem. I could not sit seriously down to write a serious romance under any other motive than to save my life; and if it were indispensable for me to keep it up and never relax into laughing at myself or other people, I am sure I should be hung before I had finished the first chapter.

Excerpt from a personal letter

She ventured to hope he did not always read only poetry; and to say, that she thought it was the misfortune of poetry, to be seldom safely enjoyed by those who enjoyed it completely; and that the strong feelings which alone could estimate it truly, were the very feelings which ought to taste it but sparingly.

Persuasion

I often wonder how *you* can find time for
what you do, in addition to the care of the
house; and how good Mrs. West could have
written such books and collected so many hard
works, with all her family cares, is still more a
matter of astonishment! Composition seems
to me impossible with a head full of joints of
mutton and doses of rhubarb.

Excerpt from a personal letter

'It is only a novel . . . or, in short, only some work in which the greatest powers of the mind are displayed, in which the most thorough knowledge of human nature, the happiest delineation of its varieties, the liveliest effusions of wit and humour, are conveyed to the world in the best-chosen language.'

Northanger Abbey

Nobody could catch cold by the sea; nobody wanted appetite by the sea; nobody wanted spirits; nobody wanted strength. Sea air was healing, softening, relaxing—fortifying and bracing—seemingly just as was wanted—sometimes one, sometimes the other.

If the sea breeze failed, the seabath was
the certain corrective; and where bathing
disagreed, the sea air alone was evidently
designed by nature for the cure.

Lady Susan

'Here's harmony!' said she; 'here's repose! Here's what may leave all painting and all music behind, and what poetry only can attempt to describe! Here's what may tranquilize every care, and lift the heart to rapture!

When I look out on such a night as this, I feel as if there could be neither wickedness nor sorrow in the world; and there certainly would be less of both if the sublimity of Nature were more attended to, and people were carried more out of themselves by contemplating such a scene.'

Mansfield Park

'And so ended his affection,' said Elizabeth impatiently. 'There has been many a one, I fancy, overcome in the same way. I wonder who first discovered the efficacy of poetry in driving away love!'

'I have been used to consider poetry as the food of love,' said Darcy.

Pride and Prejudice

'Indulge your imagination in every possible flight.'

Pride and Prejudice

'How wonderful, how very wonderful the operations of time, and the changes of the human mind!'

Mansfield Park

'But for my own part, if a book is well written, I always find it too short.'

Northanger Abbey

'I declare after all there is no enjoyment like reading! How much sooner one tires of anything than of a book! When I have a house of my own, I shall be miserable if I have not an excellent library.'

Pride and Prejudice

'Oh! write, write. Finish it at once.
Let there be an end of this suspense.
Fix, commit, condemn yourself.'

Mansfield Park

No, I must keep to my own style and go on in my own way; and though I may never succeed again in that, I am convinced that I should totally fail in any other.

Excerpt from a personal letter

'The person, be it gentleman or lady,
who has not pleasure in a good novel,
must be intolerably stupid.'

Northanger Abbey

'He admires as a lover, not as a connoisseur. To satisfy me, those characters must be united. I could not be happy with a man whose taste did not in every point coincide with my own. He must enter into all my feelings; the same books, the same music must charm us both.'

Sense and Sensibility

'A person who can write a long letter with ease, cannot write ill.'

Pride and Prejudice

'If any one faculty of our nature may be called more wonderful than the rest, I do think it is memory. There seems something more speakingly incomprehensible in the powers, the failures, the inequalities of memory, than in any other of our intelligences.

'The memory is sometimes so retentive,

so serviceable, so obedient; at others, so
bewildered and so weak; and at others again,
so tyrannic, so beyond control! We are, to be
sure, a miracle in every way; but our powers
of recollecting and of forgetting do seem
peculiarly past finding out.'

Mansfield Park

If a rainy morning deprived them of other enjoyments, they were still resolute in meeting in defiance of wet and dirt, and shut themselves up, to read novels together.

Northanger Abbey

'Let us never underestimate the power of a well-written letter.'

Persuasion

'I am delighted with the book! I should like to spend my whole life in reading it. I assure you, if it had not been to meet you, I would not have come away from it for all the world.'

Northanger Abbey

'Without music, life would be a blank to me.'

Emma

'I cannot speak well enough to be unintelligible.'

Northanger Abbey

'They are much to be pitied who have not been given a taste for nature early in life.'

Mansfield Park

'How are the civilities and compliments of every day to be related as they ought to be, unless noted down every evening in a journal?'

Northanger Abbey

An artist cannot do anything slovenly.

Excerpt from a personal letter

'Of music! Then pray speak aloud. It is of all subjects my delight. I must have my share in the conversation if you are speaking of music.'

Pride and Prejudice

'[N]o excellence in music is to be acquired without constant practice.'

Pride and Prejudice

Good Manners,
Virtue, and Vice

'Sense will always have attractions for me.'

Sense and Sensibility

'My object then,' replied Darcy, 'was to show you, by every civility in my power, that I was not so mean as to resent the past; and I hoped to obtain your forgiveness, to lessen your ill opinion, by letting you see that your reproofs had been attended to.'

Pride and Prejudice

[On arriving in London:]
Here I am once more in this scene of dissipation and vice, and I begin already to find my morals corrupted.

Excerpt from a personal letter

'It has sunk him, I cannot say how much it has sunk him in my opinion. So unlike what a man should be! None of that upright integrity, that strict adherence to truth and principle, that disdain of trick and littleness, which a man should display in every transaction of his life.'

Emma

'I am tired of submitting my will to the caprices of others—of resigning my own judgment in deference to those to whom I owe no duty, and for whom I feel no respect.'

Lady Susan

The Webbs are really gone! When I saw the waggons at the door, and thought of all the trouble they must have in moving, I began to reproach myself for not having liked them better; but since the waggons have disappeared my conscience has been closed again, and I am excessively glad they are gone.

Excerpt from a personal letter

'There is hardly any personal defect which an agreeable manner might not gradually reconcile one to.'

Persuasion

'A scheme of which every part promises delight, can never be successful; and general disappointment is only warded off by the defense of some little peculiar vexation.'

Pride and Prejudice

Ben and Anna walked here . . . and she looked so pretty, it was quite a pleasure to see her, so young and so blooming, and so innocent, as if she had never had a wicked thought in her life, which yet one has some reason to suppose she must have had, if we believe the doctrine of original sin.

Excerpt from a personal letter

'The metropolis, I imagine, is a pretty fair sample of the rest.'
'Not, I should hope, of the proportion of virtue to vice throughout the kingdom. We do not look in great cities for our best morality. It is not there that respectable people of any denomination can do most good; and it certainly is not there that the influence of the clergy can be most felt.'

Mansfield Park

You deserve a longer letter than this; but it is my unhappy fate seldom to treat people so well as they deserve.

Excerpt from a personal letter

'There is one thing, Emma, which a man can always do if he chooses, and that is his duty; not by manoeuvring and finessing, but by vigour and resolution.'

Emma

'What do you know of my heart?
What do you know of anything
but your own suffering.'

Sense and Sensibility

'We have all a better guide in
ourselves, if we would attend
to it, than any other person can be.'

Mansfield Park

'We do not look in our great cities for our best morality.'

Mansfield Park

'How little of permanent happiness could belong to a couple who were only brought together because their passions were stronger than their virtue.'

Pride and Prejudice

To flatter and follow others, without being flattered and followed in turn, is but a state of half enjoyment.

Persuasion

'I was so anxious to do what is right that I forgot to do what *is* right.'

Mansfield Park

'I was given good principles, but left to follow them in pride and conceit.'

Pride and Prejudice

'Yes, vanity is a weakness indeed. But pride—where there is a real superiority of mind, pride will be always under good regulation.'

Pride and Prejudice

He was the better for ever for his illness. He had suffered, and he had learnt to think, two advantages that he had never known before; and the self-reproach arising from the deplorable event in Wimpole Street, to which he felt himself accessory by all the dangerous intimacy of his unjustifiable theatre, made an impression on his mind which . . . was durable in its happy effects.

He became what he ought to be, useful
to his father, steady and quiet, and not living
merely for himself.

Mansfield Park

'Resignation to inevitable evils is the duty of us all.'

Pride and Prejudice

'Wickedness is always wickedness, but folly is not always folly. It depends upon the character of those who handle it.'

Emma

That punishment, the public punishment of disgrace, should in a just measure attend his share of the offence, is, we know, not one of the barriers, which society gives to virtue.

In this world, the penalty is less equal than could be wished; but without presuming to look forward to a juster appointment hereafter, we may fairly consider a man of sense like Henry Crawford, to be providing for himself no small portion of vexation and regret.

Mansfield Park

'Though where so many hours have been spent in convincing myself that I am right, is there not some reason to fear I may be wrong?'

Sense and Sensibility

'Nobody minds having what is too good for them.'

Mansfield Park

'It isn't what we say or think that defines us, but what we do.'

Sense and Sensibility

She was feeling, thinking, trembling about everything; agitated, happy, miserable, infinitely obliged, absolutely angry.

Mansfield Park

'One man's ways may be as good as another's, but we all like our own best.'

Persuasion

To his foes I could wish a resemblance in fate:
  That they, too, may suffer themselves, soon or late,
The injustice they warrant. But vain is my spite
They cannot so suffer who never do right.

Excerpt from the poem 'Of A Ministry Pitiful, Angry, Mean'

'We all know him to be a proud, unpleasant sort of man; but this would be nothing if you really liked him.'

Pride and Prejudice

She was without any power, because she was without any desire of command over herself.

Sense and Sensibility

'There is, I believe, in every disposition a tendency to some particular evil—a natural defect, which not even the best education can overcome.'

Pride and Prejudice

She felt that she could so much more depend upon the sincerity of those who sometimes looked or said a careless or a hasty thing, than of those whose presence of mind never varied, whose tongue never slipped.

Persuasion

'If I could not be persuaded into doing what I thought wrong, I will never be tricked into it.'

Northanger Abbey

'Sometimes one is guided by what they say of themselves, and very frequently by what other people say of them, without giving oneself time to deliberate and judge.'

Sense and Sensibility

'Vanity working on a weak head
produces every sort of mischief.'

Emma

She hoped to be wise and reasonable in time; but alas! Alas! She must confess to herself that she was not wise yet.

Persuasion

'I will be calm. I will be mistress of myself.'

Sense and Sensibility

'How quick come the reasons for approving what we like.'

Persuasion

'Money can only give happiness where there is nothing else to give it.'

Sense and Sensibility

'Think only of the past as its
remembrance gives you pleasure.'

Pride and Prejudice

'From the very beginning—from the first moment, I may almost say—of my acquaintance with you, your manners, impressing me with the fullest belief of your arrogance, your conceit, and your selfish disdain of the feelings of others, were such as to form the groundwork of the disapprobation

on which succeeding events have built so
immovable a dislike; and I had not known you
a month before I felt that you were the last
man in the world on whom I could ever be
prevailed on to marry.'

Pride and Prejudice

'I have faults enough, but they are not, I hope, of understanding. My temper I dare not vouch for. It is, I believe, too little yielding—certainly too little for the convenience of the world. I cannot forget the follies and vices of others so soon as I ought, nor their offenses against myself.

'My feelings are not puffed about with every attempt to move them. My temper would perhaps be called resentful. My good opinion once lost, is lost forever.'

Pride and Prejudice

'Now I must give one smirk and then we may be rational again.'

Northanger Abbey

'General benevolence, but not general friendship, make a man what he ought to be.'

Emma

'I could easily forgive his pride, if he had not mortified mine.'

Pride and Prejudice

'I cannot think well of a man who sports with any woman's feelings; and there may often be a great deal more suffered than a stander-by can judge of.'

Mansfield Park

He had imagined himself indifferent, when he had only been angry; and he had been unjust to her merits, because he had been a sufferer from them.

Persuasion

'I speak what appears to me the general opinion; and where an opinion is general, it is usually correct.'

Mansfield Park

'Better be without sense than misapply it as you do.'

Emma

'Do not give way to useless alarm … though it is right to be prepared for the worst, there is no occasion to look on it as certain.'

Pride and Prejudice

'You have qualities which I had not before supposed to exist in such a degree in any human creature. You have some touches of the angel in you beyond what—not merely beyond what one sees, because one never sees anything like it—but beyond what one fancies might be.'

Mansfield Park

'It is very difficult for the prosperous to be humble.'

Emma

'Don't imagine that nobody in this house can see or judge but yourself. Don't act yourself, if you do not like it, but don't expect to govern everybody else.'

Mansfield Park

'If there is anything disagreeable going on,
men are always sure to get out of it.'

Persuasion

'Angry people are not always wise.'

Pride and Prejudice

'Every impulse of feeling should be guided by reason; and, in my opinion, exertion should always be in proportion to what is required.'

Pride and Prejudice

'Shyness is only the effect of a sense of inferiority in some way or other. If I could persuade myself that my manners were perfectly easy and graceful, I should not be shy.'

Sense and Sensibility

'Selfishness must always be forgiven, you know, because there is no hope of a cure.'

Mansfield Park

'Those who do not complain are never pitied.'

Pride and Prejudice

'. . . when pain is over, the remembrance of it often becomes a pleasure.'

Persuasion

'Nothing is more deceitful ... than the appearance of humility. It is often only carelessness of opinion, and sometimes an indirect boast.'

Pride and Prejudice

'Your defect is a propensity to hate everybody.' 'And yours,' he replied with a smile, 'is willfully to misunderstand them.'

Pride and Prejudice

'There are people, who the more you do for them, the less they will do for themselves.'

Emma

'There is a stubbornness about me that never can bear to be frightened at the will of others. My courage always rises at every attempt to intimidate me.'

Pride and Prejudice

I listen—'tis not sound alone—'tis sense,
'Tis Genius, Taste and Tenderness of Soul.
'Tis genuine warmth of heart without pretence
And purity of Mind that crowns the whole.

Excerpt from the poem 'To the Memory of Mrs. Lefroy
who died Dec. 16—my birthday'

'Respect for right conduct is felt by everybody.'

Emma

'I cannot forget the follies and vices of others so soon as I ought, nor their offenses against myself.'

Pride and Prejudice

She speaks; 'tis Eloquence—that grace of Tongue
So rare, so lovely!—Never misapplied
By her to palliate Vice, or deck a Wrong,
She speaks and reasons but on Virtue's side.

*Excerpt from the poem 'To the Memory of Mrs. Lefroy
who died Dec. 16—my birthday'*

315

'Silly things do cease to be silly if they are done by sensible people in an impudent way.'

Emma

'One cannot be always laughing at a man without now and then stumbling on something witty.'

Pride and Prejudice

Seldom, very seldom, does complete truth belong to any human disclosure; seldom can it happen that something is not a little disguised or a little mistaken.

Emma

'It is very often nothing but our own vanity that deceives us. Women fancy admiration means more than it does. And men take care that they should.'

Pride and Prejudice

'Follies and nonsense, whims and inconsistencies, do divert me, I own, and I laugh at them whenever I can.'

Pride and Prejudice

'What is right to be done cannot be
done too soon.'

Emma

'I am convinced that [pride] is very common indeed; that human nature is particularly prone to it, and that there are very few of us who do not cherish a feeling of self-complacency on the score of some quality or other, real or imaginary.'

'Vanity and pride are different things, though the words are often used synonymously. A person may be proud without being vain. Pride relates more to our opinion of ourselves; vanity, to what we would have others think of us.'

Pride and Prejudice

'The power of doing anything with quickness is always prized much by the possessor, and often without any attention to the imperfection of the performance.'

Pride and Prejudice

'A man who has nothing to do with his own time has no conscience in his intrusion on that of others.'

Sense and Sensibility

Surprises are foolish things. The pleasure is not enhanced, and the inconvenience is often considerable.

Emma

'I have not wanted syllables where actions have spoken so plainly.'

Sense and Sensibility

A Philosophy
of Life

'We have all a better guide in ourselves,
if we would attend to it, than any
other person can be.'

Mansfield Park

'I have no talent for certainty.'

Mansfield Park

Another day is now gone, and added to those, for which we were before accountable.

Excerpt from a personal prayer

'What are men to rocks and mountains?'

Pride and Prejudice

'Human nature is so well disposed towards those who are in interesting situations, that a young person, who either marries or dies, is sure of being kindly spoken of.'

Emma

'I thought it all over, and in spite of the shame of being so much older, felt with thankfulness that I was quite as happy now as then.'

Excerpt from a personal letter

'A very narrow income has a tendency to contract the mind, and sour the temper.'

Emma

'But indeed I would rather have nothing but tea.'

Mansfield Park

'Till this moment I never knew myself.'

Pride and Prejudice

'I wish, as well as everybody else, to be
perfectly happy; but, like everybody else,
it must be in my own way.'

Sense and Sensibility

'Oh! Do not attack me with your watch.
A watch is always too fast or too slow.
I cannot be dictated to by a watch.'

Mansfield Park

'Let us have the luxury of silence.'

Mansfield Park

'I had a very pleasant evening, however,
though you will probably find out that
there was no particular reason for it; but I do
not think it worth while to wait for enjoyment
until there is some real opportunity for it.'

Excerpt from a personal letter

'What wild imaginations one forms
where dear self is concerned!
How sure to be mistaken!'

Persuasion

'There is something so amiable in the prejudices of a young mind, that one is sorry to see them give way to the reception of more general opinions.'

Sense and Sensibility

'Let other pens dwell on guilt and misery. I quit such odious subjects as soon as I can, impatient to restore everybody not greatly in fault themselves to tolerable comfort, and to have done with all the rest.'

Mansfield Park

'If things are going untowardly one month, they are sure to mend the next.'

Emma

'Money can only give happiness where
there is nothing else to give it.'

Sense and Sensibility

'[W]here other powers of entertainment are wanting, the true philosopher will derive benefit from such as are given.'

Pride and Prejudice

'Time will explain.'

Persuasion

'You see the evil, but you do not see the consolation. There will be little rubs and disappointments everywhere, and we are all apt to expect too much; but then, if one scheme of happiness fails, human nature turns to another; if the first calculation is wrong, we make a second better: we find comfort somewhere.'

Mansfield Park

'It was, perhaps, one of those cases in which advice is good or bad only as the event decides.'

Persuasion

I cannot help thinking that it is more natural to have flowers grow out of the head than fruit.

Excerpt from a personal letter

'You must be the best judge of your own happiness.'

Emma

The Complete
Works of Jane Austen

Austen's novels published during her lifetime

Sense and Sensibility (1811)

Pride and Prejudice (1813)

Mansfield Park (1814)

Emma (1815)

Austen's posthumously published novels

Persuasion (1817)

Northanger Abbey (1817)

Lady Susan (1871)

Unfinished novels

The Watsons (1804)

Sanditon (1817)

Other works

Sir Charles Grandison (adapted play) (1793, 1800)

Plan of a Novel (1815)

Poems (1796–1817)

Prayers (1796–1817)

Letters (1796–1817)

Austen's youthful writings, the 'Juvenilia'

Volume the First (1787–1793)

Frederic & Elfrida

Jack & Alice

Edgar & Emma

Henry and Eliza

The Adventures of Mr. Harley

About the Compiler

Andrea Kirk Assaf lives between a rural homestead in Remus, Michigan, and the Villa Magnolia in Rome, Italy. Along with her family, she hosts students, pilgrims, and countless dinner guests in the Eternal City. She has compiled five other books in the Little Book of Wisdom series (2008–present), and is the author of *The Honey Book* (2021).

Reader's Journal

May we now, and on each return of night, consider how the past day has been spent by us, what have been our prevailing thoughts, words, and actions during it.

Excerpt from a personal prayer

In the pages that follow, dear reader, we invite you to reflect on Jane Austen's words of wisdom and wit, and record any thoughts or inclinations towards what you have read.

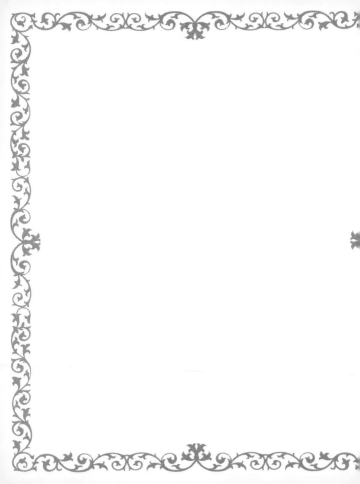

Other titles in the
LITTLE BOOK OF WISDOM series:

JESUS'
LITTLE BOOK
OF WISDOM
ISBN: 978-0-00-826224-2

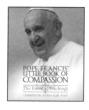

POPE FRANCIS'
LITTLE BOOK
OF COMPASSION
ISBN: 978-0-00-819317-1

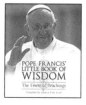

POPE FRANCIS'
LITTLE BOOK
OF WISDOM
ISBN: 978-0-00-794744-7

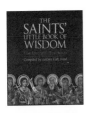

THE SAINTS'
LITTLE BOOK
OF WISDOM
ISBN: 978-0-00-795456-8

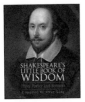

SHAKESPEARE'S
LITTLE BOOK
OF WISDOM
ISBN: 978-0-00-795485-8

C.S. LEWIS'
LITTLE BOOK
OF WISDOM
ISBN: 978-0-00-828247-9